WOL

Please return/renew this item by the last date shown.
Library items may also be renewed by phone on
030 33 33 1234 (24hours) or via our website

www.cumbria.gov.uk/libraries

Cumbria Libraries

CLIC
Interactive Catalogue

Ask for a CLIC password

Fairy
Unicorns

Frost Fair

Zanna Davidson

Illustrated by Nuno Alexandre Vieira

Meet the Unicorns

Zoe

Astra

Sorrel

Unicorn King

Eirra

Orion

Lily

Shadow

Unicorn Island

The White Mountains

Mount Flores

Island of Flowers

WESTERN SEA

Cave

Moon River

Flower Meadows

Cave

Rose Bower

Moon River

Fairtree Forest

Underwater Palace

Silvery Glade

Entrance from the Great Oak

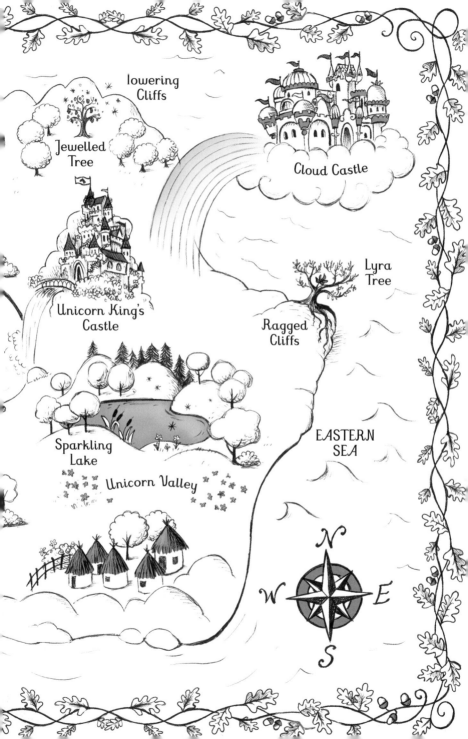

Towering
Cliffs

Jewelled
Tree

Cloud Castle

Unicorn King's
Castle

Lyra
Tree

Ragged
Cliffs

Sparkling
Lake

Unicorn Valley

EASTERN
SEA

N
W   E
S

Contents

Chapter One

Zoe pulled on a thick woolly jumper over her pyjamas and gazed out of her bedroom window. Outside, the moon was full and the night was cold and clear. She had never stayed with Great-Aunt May in winter before and everything looked very different. The oak tree at the end of the garden stood tall and bare against the dark sky, and a covering of

frost lay over the tangled lawn. Zoe waited a
moment, making sure the house was quiet.
Then she picked up her rucksack, slipped on

her fleecy
winter boots
and tiptoed
out through
the back door.

The crisp
air swept over
her as she
raced down the path.
Hidden within the oak tree
was Unicorn Island, a secret world full of
fairy unicorns. Zoe hadn't visited the island
since her summer holidays and now, finally,
she was able to go back.

When she reached the foot of the tree, Zoe pulled a tiny silver bag out of her pocket. Delicately, she took a pinch of magical dust. As she sprinkled it over herself, she chanted the words of a spell:

Let me pass into the magic tree,
Where *fairy* unicorns *fly* wild and *free*.
Show me the trail of sparkling light,
To Unicorn Island, shining bright.

At once, there was a fizzing and a tingling that started in her toes and her fingertips. Then she was shrinking down, down, down, until she was no bigger than the blades of grass around her. Zoe let out a whoop of joy. She was fairy-sized again!

She took off at a run, heading along the
narrow tunnel between the oak tree's roots,
following a path of glimmering light. A trail
of frost sparkled beneath her feet and her
breath came out in tiny clouds of mist.
At last, she rounded a corner and caught
her first wintry glimpse of Unicorn Island at
the end of the tunnel…

Before her lay a white world. The trees in the Silvery Glade dazzled against the brightness of the snow. Beautiful icicles hung from the branches and their rainbow leaves were covered in shimmering frost. Beyond the glade, the gently sloping hills of Unicorn Valley caught the sunlight and between them wound Moon River, a glittering ribbon of ice.

She heard muffled hoof beats and looked over to see her friend, Astra, galloping through the trees towards her.

Her pearly horn gleamed, her creamy coat making her nearly invisible but for the sprinkling of silvery stars along her back. Her gossamer-light fairy wings were fluttering with excitement.

"Zoe!" she cried. "I'm so happy to see you again. I knew you wouldn't be back until winter, and I was so excited when the first snow fell, knowing you'd come soon."

Zoe flung her arms around Astra's neck, loving the feel of her silky, soft coat against her skin.

"I've missed you," she said. "I'm so glad to be back here again." She gazed around for a moment. "And to be here in winter!" she added. "Unicorn Island looks so beautiful in the snow."

"I know!" said Astra, with a little shiver. "Although this winter has been colder and longer than ever before. You've come at a good time, though. It's the Frost Fair on Moon River today! We have one every year. It's our winter festival."

"Ooh!" said Zoe. "What happens at the Frost Fair?"

"There are fairground rides, skating on the

ice, music and dancing. As well as the most delicious food!" said Astra excitedly. "Hot chestnuts, frosted candyfloss and honey mead. Would you like to come?"

Zoe nodded. "I'd love to," she said. "But first…I brought something for you." She slipped off her rucksack and reached inside it, pulling out a fleecy blanket covered in stars. "I made this for you," said Zoe. "I hoped it might keep you warm in the snow."

"Wow!" said Astra. "It's gorgeous."

Zoe laid it over Astra's back and the little unicorn smiled. "I'm never going to take it off," she said.

"It's so cosy." She bent her legs as she spoke so that Zoe could swing herself onto her back. "Now," she said. "Let's fly to the Frost Fair!"

Zoe wrapped her arms around Astra's neck and they galloped out of the Silvery Glade, snow spraying up behind them. Then, as the trees began to thin, Astra stretched out her wings and the next moment they were soaring over the valley. The cold wind whistled through Astra's hair and Zoe could feel her skin tingle with the chill of the breeze.

"It all looks so peaceful," she said to Astra.

"I know," Astra replied. "Not like before, when Shadow sent the winds and the floods."

Zoe shivered at the memory. Shadow was an evil fairy pony from an island across the sea, who was desperate to control Unicorn

Island. If he succeeded, then by law the
Unicorn King would have failed in his task to
protect the island, and Shadow would be free
to rule in his place unchallenged.

"There's been no sign of him," Astra went
on. "We can only hope he's given up and gone
away. But let's not think of Shadow today.
I want us to enjoy the Frost Fair."

"You're right," said Zoe, grinning. "I'm not
going to let anything ruin it!"

She looked down and realized they were
already flying over Moon River, its glittering
surface as smooth and clear as glass. "How
far is the Frost Fair from here?" she asked.

"Not far," Astra replied. "It's on the banks of
Moon River, beneath the Unicorn King's Castle.
It should be coming into view any moment."

Zoe's gaze followed the winding path of the river until, in the distance, she glimpsed the castle. Carved into the rock face, in summer the castle had seemed a living part of the landscape, cloaked in moss and tumbling ivy, almost hidden from view. But now she could see it in all its beauty – its shining marble walls, its turrets topped with snow. Jutting out beneath it was a waterfall, frozen into thousands of glittering ice-crystals, sparkling in the morning sun.

"There's the Frost Fair!" cried Zoe. "I see it now."

Beneath the Unicorn King's Castle, dotting the edges of the river, were dozens of little stalls. A band was playing lively tunes and behind the stalls on one side was a brightly lit

fairground. The fair thronged with unicorns
– riding on the carousel, skating on the ice.
Hot drinks bubbled above roaring fires and
the delicious smell of roasting chestnuts filled
the air.

"Oh, look over there!" gasped Zoe, pointing
at a huge big wheel carved from ice, with
unicorns riding round in prettily painted
baskets. "It looks so fun!" she cried. "Can
you fly any faster?" she added with
a laugh. "I can't wait!"

Chapter Two

In no time at all, Astra's beating wings had
brought them above the Unicorn King's
Castle and from there she began to swoop
down towards the riverbank, landing in a
heap of powdery snow. Zoe slid from her back,
waggling her fingers and stamping her feet to
warm them after the chill of the ride.

"What shall we do first?" asked Zoe.

"I want to try the big wheel, and the carousel. Oh! And there's a big dipper. And I can't wait to skate on the ice as well…"

Astra laughed. "Can we eat first?" she asked. "All this cold air is making me hungry."

"Definitely!" said Zoe, as she caught the delicious scent of hot honey mead and glimpsed stalls of brightly coloured sweets.

"Let's try everything!" Astra grinned, excitedly.

They wandered from stall to stall, feasting on toffee apples, hot potatoes and sweet nut clusters. Zoe tasted the frosted candyfloss and sipped honey mead and creamy hot chocolate brimming with melted marshmallows.

"Oh!" said Zoe, as they reached the last stall. "I don't think I've got any room for roasted chestnuts."

"Take some for later," suggested Astra. "They're so delicious. I'd hate for you to leave without trying them."

"Great idea," said Zoe, quickly popping some into her bag. "What shall we do now?"

As she spoke she gazed over at the river, where more and more unicorns were spilling onto its frozen surface. The banks were lined with ice skates, and each unicorn was slipping them on over their hoofs, before gliding onto the river's smooth, glassy surface. The unicorns looked so beautiful, fluttering their gossamer-light wings to speed them on their way, their manes and tails streaming out behind them.

"Do you want to try skating?" asked Astra, following her gaze. "It's almost as much fun as flying. Then we can save the rides for last."

"I'd love that," said Zoe.

"Then follow me!" said Astra.

She cantered over to the river, where she slipped her hoofs into the special skates.

"Oh, but I don't have any skates," said Zoe, looking longingly at the sweep of icy river.

"I'm sure we can do something about that," said a unicorn behind her. Zoe turned to see Magus, an old unicorn with a long wispy beard and wise, dark eyes. He pointed his gleaming horn at her feet and suddenly, in a shower of sparkles, she was wearing a perfect pair of ice skates. "Oh! Thank you!" Zoe said, hardly able to believe her luck.

Then they were off, skating across the ice, weaving in and out of the other unicorns, twirling and racing, the wind whistling through Zoe's hair. "You're right!" she said. "This almost feels like flying."

Her glance darted left and right as she skated, drinking in the beautiful, glittering white landscape as it flashed past, the merry

tunes of the Frost Fair band thrumming in her

ears. The other unicorns smiled as she passed

them, or called out her name in greeting,

and Zoe waved back.

High above, she could hear the excited cries of young unicorns on the big wheel, while others shrieked with glee as they shot down the helter-skelter. Zoe hoped she would remember this moment for ever.

They skated on until Astra came to a halt at the bend in the river. "Over there!" said Astra. "I can see my mother and the other Guardians."

Zoe looked over and waved excitedly. There was Sorrel, Astra's mother, Guardian of the Trees. Beside her stood Lily, Guardian of the Flowers and Nimbus, Guardian of the Clouds and the Unicorn King himself.

"They're usually hard at work, caring for the island," said Astra. "But everyone comes to celebrate winter at the Frost Fair."

Together, Astra and Zoe skated over to say hello.

"Welcome back, Zoe," said Sorrel, in her gentle voice. "It's lovely to see you today. You look as if you're enjoying the Frost Fair."

"Greetings," added the Unicorn King. "It's good to have you among us. Will you be taking part in the ice sculpture competition? Eirra is arriving later to judge it, so there's still time to enter."

Zoe looked questioningly at Astra.

"Oh, I forgot!" said Astra. "It's another part of the Frost Fair. All the unicorns make ice sculptures and then Eirra, Guardian of the Snow, chooses the winner. He's the strictest of the Guardians," she added in a whisper. "But he's always fair."

Sorrel smiled down at them both. "If you want to enter you'd better hurry," she said. "Most of the unicorns have already started — look over there, next to the fairground."

Zoe saw unicorns standing alone, or in pairs, carving blocks of ice with their horns. She glimpsed beautiful shapes — a swan, a flying unicorn, a towering tree.

"Then what are we waiting for?" said Zoe, turning to Astra. "Let's begin."

They found a spot a little way from the other unicorns, and set to work. Zoe and Astra became so absorbed in their task that they didn't even notice the light snow which had started to fall. Zoe was vaguely aware of the other unicorns around them, quietly making sculptures of their own. But everything had become very still and very quiet. Finally, she looked up. Their ice sculpture was almost finished. They had tried to make one of the Unicorn King's Castle.

"Oh dear," laughed Zoe. "I'm not sure we're going to win. I'm not even sure it's clearly a castle. The turrets look more like spikes. In fact, it looks a lot like… a hedgehog."

"You could be right," said Astra, stepping back to look at it properly. "Maybe we should pretend it's *meant* to be a hedgehog. A snowy hedgehog," she added, as a fat snowflake landed on the top of the sculpture.

"That's odd," said Zoe, gazing at it. "It's almost as if the snowflake has a purple glow. Are snowflakes always like that here?"

She held out her hand as she spoke and caught another one as it drifted past. Zoe watched in amazement as it popped open, a purple liquid seeping across her palm.

"Wow," said Astra, a puzzled frown creasing her brow. "I've never seen one like that before."

Suddenly, there was a shout from the sky. They both looked up to see Eirra, Guardian of the Snow, in the distance. He was swooping down from the White Mountains across the river, his wings pulled back as he gathered speed.

"Take cover!" he cried. "Hurry! Do it now!"

"On to my back," cried Astra.

Zoe leaped astride her and they galloped
back towards the Frost Fair. She was vaguely
aware of ice sculptures glittering all around
them, and the sound of hoof beats as other
unicorns joined them, all rushing to take
shelter under the stalls.

"What's going on?" asked one unicorn.

"I don't know," panted Astra.

But before they could say more, Eirra was

standing before them, chanting frantically.

Keep the unicorns safe from harm,
From the snowflakes' evil charm.
With this dazzling sparkle shower,
Stop the snowflakes' evil power.

Tiny silver stars appeared, shimmering and dazzling in a magical cloud that had enveloped them all by the end of the spell.

Zoe could feel her skin tingling as the starry cloud swept over her, and then the air just around them was clear once more. The spell stopped the snowflakes from touching them.

"What's happening? Why do we need protecting?" asked Astra.

There was a chorus of cries from the other

unicorns. "I don't understand! What's going on? Can you tell us?"

Eirra glanced outside their circle at the falling snow. "It's the purple snowflakes," he explained, deep frown lines etched across his brow. "They're enchanted. Every time one touches a unicorn, the unicorn turns to ice."

"No! It can't be true," said another unicorn, his face turning pale with shock.

"We were out in the snow for ages," said another, her voice filled with disbelief. "Why haven't we been turned to ice?"

"You were safe under the trees," Eirra replied. "As a human, Zoe was safe from the spell. Astra, you're lucky you were wearing that blanket. If a snowflake had touched your legs or your head, you too would have been frozen. Just look around you…"

At his words, the unicorns turned to look out at the Frost Fair. Through the curtain of falling snow, they could see Eirra was telling the truth.

"I can see the statues," whispered Zoe. "The king…the Guardians…all the others… Look!"

Her voice broke as she took in the scene before her. It was just as Eirra had said. All the other unicorns, apart from the small crowd gathered between the stalls, had been turned to ice.

"Frozen!" Astra sobbed beside her. "They've all been frozen."

Chapter Three

In shock, Zoe, Astra and the few other
unicorns that were left could only gaze at the
terrible scene before them. There were
unicorns everywhere, frozen in the moment
they were touched by the purple snowflakes.
Some were mid-leap over Moon River, others
were caught drinking honey mead or eating a
chestnut, their glassy stillness making them

look like ice sculptures. A little way beyond, on the very edge of the riverbank, stood the Unicorn King. His face looked grim and his body was reared up, as if to fight off the wicked spell.

Only a little while ago the Frost Fair had been alive with laughter and chatter, as unicorns milled among the stalls and skated

on the ice. Now it was a silent, eerie scene.

"My spell will protect you from the enchanted snowflakes," said Eirra. "But I was too late to help the others."

Zoe watched helplessly as the remaining unicorns ran from statue to statue, calling out to each one to try and break the spell. Astra

rushed to the frozen figure of Sorrel and began to nuzzle her, as if hoping that the warmth of her own body would melt the ice covering her.

There were tears in Astra's eyes. "Mother!" she called. "Wake up!"

Zoe ran after her friend and saw close up that Sorrel was covered in a sparkling icy sheen – both beautiful and horrifying. From beneath the ice, her eyes stared out blankly, unseeing.

"I'm afraid that's not going to help," Eirra

told Astra, as he came to join them. "The spell cast by the snowflakes is more than just a layer of ice. They freeze everything they touch to the very core."

Silent tears were now sliding down Astra's cheeks as she gazed mournfully at her mother. "This is one of Shadow's spells, isn't it?" she said bitterly. "What can we do? We must be able to do *something*."

Eirra called to the other unicorns, and they all gathered round again to hear what he had to say.

"Shadow and his helper Orion must have used the Grimoire, the ancient spell book, to find magic as deep and dark as this. It is going to take a powerful force to undo it. Not only that," he went on. "These purple snowflakes also freeze the ground, the trees and the flowers, so that it is always winter. No spring sunshine will be able to thaw them. And if Unicorn Island stays frozen too long, the king will have failed to protect the island, and Shadow will be able to take his place."

"How…how long have we got?" stammered Astra. "Before Shadow can take over the island?"

For a moment, Eirra didn't answer. Then, with a deep breath, he said, "Until dawn. That is Unicorn Law. If the king has failed to unfreeze the island by then, a new ruler must take his place."

"Isn't there a way to stop the spell, or reverse it?" asked Astra. "We can't let Shadow win. We can't leave everyone frozen…"

"There may be something we can do," said Eirra. "Have you heard of the Fire Comet?"

"What's that?" asked Zoe.

"It is a comet spoken of in the legends of the Snow Unicorns. It burns with a bright and magical flame and if caught, it can be used to help the island, whenever winter has lasted too long. The comet's flame is said to have the power to thaw the land and welcome in spring. But there is a catch – only the bravest and most pure of heart can capture it, and it cannot be controlled by magic. If the legends are true... then the comet could be just what we need."

"How do we catch it?" asked another unicorn, nervously fluttering his wings.

"We'll have to try flying up to the stars with a net," Eirra explained. "The comet travels in a circle, high in the night sky."

Eirra looked around at the anxious unicorns.

"I'll need help," he said, sternly. "Do I have any volunteers?"

Zoe could tell by the tone of his voice that the Guardian of the Snow wasn't used to being refused. She looked back at the other unicorns, but no one spoke. Her gaze caught Astra's and she knew they were both thinking the same thing – that they were willing to go, but unsure if they were up to the task.

An old unicorn was the first to speak up. "I'm not sure my wings will take me that far," he said. "I'm worried I'd slow you down – I'm not as fast as I once was. I'm sorry."

"I don't want to leave my children," said another, nodding towards the unicorn twins at her side. "Otherwise I'd go."

"I'm just too scared," admitted a third. "I've never flown up to the stars. It's so high."

After that there was silence. Zoe looked over at Astra again and this time saw a gathering look of determination in her eyes. The unicorn leaned over and whispered to her.

"Would you come with me?" she asked. "Someone has to go. We've faced dangers before. We could do this."

"Do you think?" asked Zoe.

"To be honest, I don't know," Astra replied. "But I've been thinking of my mother and I *have* to do something to help save her. I couldn't bear to be down here, waiting. We can't let Eirra go alone if he needs help."

Zoe took a deep breath. "Then of course I'll come with you," she said.

Astra turned to Eirra. "Zoe and I will be your volunteers," she said. "I know we're young, but we've fought Shadow before, and been into volcanoes and cursed palaces. We can fly up to the night sky, Eirra," she added quietly.

"But I'm worried about your magic," said the Snow Guardian in an undertone. "I know it doesn't always work, Astra. Your mother has told me..."

"But it's always worked when I'm with Zoe," Astra insisted. "And it's starting to work when I'm on my own as well."

"And when it does work, it's very powerful," added Zoe.

Eirra looked again at the small, silent group of unicorns. "Astra, Zoe, you are very brave," he said. "You may come with me. I just hope I can keep you safe. Everyone else, please go back to your homes. This night will be a cold one. You must stay warm. You are safe from the enchanted snow, but who knows what the dawn will bring…"

Chapter Four

Zoe and Astra waited by the Frost Fair for night to fall.

"I'll leave you briefly," Eirra had told them. "I must go to the Unicorn King's Castle first to fetch a star net, so that we can catch the comet. I'll be back before the first star lights the sky."

And as soon as darkness began to creep

over the island, cloaking the eerie statues, Eirra returned, just as he'd promised.

"Are you ready?" he asked them. "The stars are beginning to come out now. It's time for us to take to the skies."

"I'm ready," Astra replied, her voice steady. Without another word, Zoe climbed onto Astra's back and wrapped her arms around her neck.

"Are you going to be warm enough, Zoe?" Astra asked. "I don't feel the cold under my blanket, and my coat is thick. But it'll be cold up there, among the stars."

"I'll be fine," Zoe replied, but she couldn't hide the tremor in her voice. She'd never stayed this late on Unicorn Island before. Every time she'd visited, she'd always gone home before nightfall – Sorrel and the Unicorn King had always urged her to leave and return to her own world before morning came, but she didn't know why. Would she be trapped on Unicorn Island if she stayed until daybreak? Even as she worried, Zoe knew she had no choice. She had to stay and help the unicorns.

"I'll be fine," she said, summoning up a smile. "Your body will give me warmth and I have my thick jumper on. I'm ready for this – I really am."

"Then let's go," said Eirra, and he began fluttering his gossamer-light wings. Astra streamed after him, beating her wings in time. Zoe had to hold on tight as they shot steeply into the sky, rising at such a sharp

angle she knew
that if she let
go, she
would have
slid straight off
Astra's back.

The higher they flew,
the colder the air
became. Zoe had to
bury her fingers in
Astra's silky, soft
mane. Glancing down,
she could see Unicorn Island
getting smaller and smaller below
them, until it disappeared from view.

"Are you okay?" Zoe whispered to Astra.
"Not too tired?"

"No," Astra replied. "Although I've never flown this high before. It's strange, isn't it, being up here? It's almost like being in another world. It's so quiet…and *empty*."

Zoe nodded in agreement. There was only black sky and stars as far as the eye could see.

After that they flew on, saying nothing for a while. Zoe knew they were both wondering if they'd find the comet – and if they did, would they be able to capture it and save the island, and all the frozen unicorns?

Ahead of them, Eirra's wings never seemed to falter and when he forged too far ahead, they could still make him out – his snowflake circlet glinting in the dark sky. At last he stopped, gazing up at the stars above them and scanning the sky for signs of movement.

Zoe and Astra joined him, hovering by his side.

"It's so vast up here," said Astra. "How will we ever find the comet?"

"I've taken us north over the island," Eirra explained. "In winter, this is where you'd expect to see the Fire Comet. We're just coming into its range. We should wait here for a little while, and then if it doesn't come, head on further north. But at least it shouldn't be hard to miss. It burns with a magical blue flame. Just keep your eyes peeled."

"Oh!" cried Astra suddenly. "I can see something coming towards us! Only it doesn't look like a comet. More like another unicorn…"

Eirra whipped round to follow her gaze.

"Oh no!" he said.
"I know that
unicorn! It's Orion!"

"Wh-what's he
doing here?" Zoe
stuttered.

"Shadow must have sent him to stop us
from catching the comet," Eirra replied.

"I thought Orion couldn't come to Unicorn
Island," said Astra. "Didn't the king cast a
banishment spell?"

"He did," said Eirra, grimly. "But I should
have realized – we're so high, the banishment
spell won't work up here."

Zoe could see the huge dark shape of Orion
coming closer and closer towards them. "Then

what do we do now?" she asked. "Can we outfly him?"

Eirra shook his head and spoke quickly. "You two go on. The comet is our priority but I'll have to stay behind to deal with Orion. Here, Zoe, take the net," he added, pulling it from the bag around his neck and handing it to her. "Whatever happens, don't come back for me – just find that comet."

"Are you sure?" asked Zoe.

"Yes!" said Eirra. "Now go! Find the Fire Comet. I'll hold Orion at bay. Keep flying north. If I don't come after you, I'll meet you back in the valley."

Even as he spoke, Orion emerged from the darkness, his powerful wings scything through the air. Orion was muttering a spell beneath his breath and, a moment later, a fireball came hurtling towards them.

With a spell of his own, Eirra sent it tumbling from the sky and retaliated with a lightning bolt which shot from his horn, aimed straight at Orion.

Astra and Zoe could only watch, dazed by the speed of it all, as Orion dodged the bolt at the last minute and with an evil smile, sent a flurry of fiery hailstones back at Eirra.

Glancing round, Eirra caught sight of them both. "Go, I tell you!"

"Okay," said Astra, taking a deep breath. "Ready, Zoe?"

"Ready," Zoe replied.

Astra shot upwards at full speed,

flying high over the heads of the battling unicorns. Orion looked up and made as if to follow, but there was a shout from Eirra. "Not so fast, Orion," he called. "Take this!"

Looking over her shoulder, Zoe saw Orion turn as Eirra charged forwards, his breath billowing before him as a cloud of choking smoke.

"Do we need to go back?" asked Astra.

"We can't," said Zoe. "He told us not to. We have to find the comet. We just have to hope Eirra's magic is stronger."

The two unicorns were tumbling through the sky now in a deadly game of chase, hurling lightning bolts and burning rocks back and forth between them, dodging and racing, spinning through the stars.

Astra took one last look, then flew on until Orion and Eirra had disappeared from view. Both Zoe and Astra looked in every direction, desperately searching the sky for any sign of a blue light. Astra beat her wings as fast as she could, but however hard they looked, there was no sign of the comet.

"How far do you think we should keep flying north?" Zoe asked. "Eirra didn't mention that part…"

In reply, Astra came to a halt, fluttering in one spot. "Oh no," she said.

"What is it?"

"I don't *know* which way we're heading," said Astra. "I've… I've lost my bearings. I was so busy looking for the comet…"

"I was looking for the comet too," Zoe

replied. "I thought *you* knew where we were going."

"Well, I don't," said Astra. Her voice sounded almost snappish. Zoe gasped – she had never seen Astra like this before. Her unicorn friend was always the calm, sensible one. She never usually panicked, or got confused.

"What are you saying?" Zoe asked.

But Astra didn't reply. She was gazing at the stars around them. Everything was very still and very quiet.

"It's all so confusing," Astra whispered. "I barely even know which way is up and which way is down. I think we're lost," she said at last. "We're lost, Zoe! We're lost among the stars."

Chapter Five

"We can't be lost," said Zoe. But even as she spoke, she knew she sounded as panicked as Astra. "Unicorn Island is depending on us to find that comet. I've just realized… It's all down to us now…"

Her voice trembled as she realized the full importance of the task ahead of them.

"And my mum," added Astra quietly.

"Without the comet, my mother could be frozen for ever."

"We're not going to let that happen," said Zoe, hoping that by saying it, she could make it true.

"It's just that everything is so vast and empty…" Astra went on, sounding a little bewildered. "It makes me lose track of where we are. And being up here… It's somehow worse than being trapped down a volcano, or searching a cursed palace…"

"But we can't give up," said Zoe. "Time is running out. We only have until dawn."

"I know that," said Astra, her voice unsteady, tears of frustration filling her eyes. "But which way *is* north?"

"Okay," said Zoe. "Let's think about this. Have you ever used the stars to guide you?"

"Well, the older unicorns do," said Astra. "But I've never really flown at night and I haven't properly learned about the stars yet. Sometimes my mother—" Her voice choked on the word, and then she carried on. "My mother has often pointed them out, but it all looks so different from up here."

"Can't we summon the comet with magic?"

Astra shook her head. "Only the pure of heart can find the comet. It cannot be controlled by magic. That's what Eirra said."

Zoe could tell that Astra was working herself up into a panic. Her wings were fluttering fast, and Zoe could feel her heartbeat racing under her soft coat. She had to find a way to calm her.

"Think of your mother," she said. "She taught you so well. I *know* you can do this, Astra."

Astra took a deep breath and looked around them again. This time, the stars didn't seem like such a confusing, dazzling mass of light. She glanced at one after another, noting their size, their shape, the strength of their glow, until they formed a

pattern in her mind.

"That star there," she said at last, pointing with her horn. "The small bright star, with the cold white light – the one that shines brighter than the rest? I'm sure I've seen it before. It lies to the north of the island. If we head towards that, we should be heading towards the comet."

Zoe tried to accustom her eyes to the small bright star, so it stood out from all the others.

"Yes I can see it," she said. "Are you sure that's the one?"

"Yes I'm sure," said Astra, her voice sounding more certain. Zoe breathed a huge sigh of relief. This sounded more like her friend.

"We can do this!" Astra continued. "This time I'll keep my eyes fixed on the north star, if you search for the comet."

Zoe could only hope that they found the comet soon. She knew Astra must be starting to tire. It felt like they'd been flying for hours up here in this starlit world, and there was nowhere for Astra to stop and take rest.

Then suddenly, in the distance, there was a faint flickering of blue.

"I think I can see it!" Zoe cried in excitement. "Over there! Look below the white star – at that blue light coming towards us."

"Yes!" cried Astra. "That must be the comet. Quick, Zoe. Have you got the net?"

"I have!" said Zoe, unable to stop smiling. She gripped the star net tightly in her hand as Astra flew fast towards the comet. The closer they came, the more beautiful it seemed. The comet's head was a burning ball of fiery blue, flickering and glimmering among the stars. Behind it was a starry trail of dazzling light, like a sparkler on fireworks night – the comet's tail.

"Here's the plan," said Astra. "I'll fly alongside it, and you can lean down and grab it in the net."

The comet was moving so fast it was nearly in front of them now.

"Ready?" said Astra.

"I'm ready," said Zoe.

As they rushed towards the comet, Zoe reached down with her net, holding it firmly, her eyes fixed on its burning flame.

"Any second now… Go!" cried Astra, brushing past the fiery ball on beating wings. But just as Zoe leaned down to scoop it from the sky, it turned and twisted, zigzagging out of the way.

"Oh!" cried Zoe. "It doesn't want to be caught!"

"Well we're not leaving without it," said Astra. She dived down after the comet, her wings swishing, her mane and tail streaming out behind her.

She zigzagged after the comet, gaining

speed until she was hovering above it. "I'm
going to drop down. Can you catch it from
above?"

"I think so," said Zoe.

But just as Astra plummeted towards it, the
comet turned again, this time sailing past

them in a
series of
sparkling loops.
They chased the comet
through the stars, barely stopping to
catch their breath. Sometimes it would halt,
almost as if it was waiting for them, and then
dart away at the last moment. Zoe couldn't
help thinking it was as if the comet were
enjoying having an audience, a chance to
show off all its tricks. It would dive up
and down, weave around them
in circles, jump from star
to star.

"Oh!"
cried Astra,
as the comet darted away from them one

more time, letting Zoe's net brush along its tail, teasing them. "I'm not sure how much longer I can keep going. My wings are beginning to ache with tiredness."

"Oh, Astra," said Zoe. "You must be exhausted. But we must capture it."

"I know," said Astra, her voice breaking. "Too much depends on this. The island…my mother…"

"We must be doing something wrong," said Zoe.

Astra watched the comet, weaving above them. "It's not like it's racing away from us. It's more as if it's playing a game."

She fell silent, her brow furrowed in thought. "Maybe we shouldn't be chasing it at all? Maybe it should just come to us?"

"Well that's about the only thing we haven't tried," said Zoe.

"Right," said Astra, decisively. "I'm going to hover in this spot. Let's be patient and see if it comes."

Zoe held out her net and Astra hovered on fluttering wings. Slowly, tantalizingly, the comet looped back and made its way towards them.

"I feel this is our last chance," whispered Astra.

The comet was within touching distance now. Close up, Zoe could see inside its fiery blue ball, where a golden light flickered and crackled. It stopped above the net, thrumming and buzzing, its tail flicking from side to side like some kind of magical starry fish.

Zoe and Astra both held their breaths.
Then a moment later, with a whispered sigh,
the comet fell like a ripe peach, straight into
the outstretched net.

Chapter Six

"We've done it!" whooped Zoe. "We've caught the comet. Unicorn Island is saved!"

"I can hardly believe it," said Astra. "Just when I thought I couldn't go on…"

Keeping a careful hold on the net, Zoe leaned forward to hug Astra. "You were amazing," she said. "I don't know how you've kept flying this long."

"We'd better head back," said Astra. "We have to release the comet across the island before dawn. It feels like we've been up here for hours. I just hope we can get back in time!"

With those words, Astra stretched out her wings and began whooshing back down through the stars. Zoe gazed at the comet glowing in her net, its starry tail gently flickering. But at a sudden cry from Astra, she looked up.

"A unicorn! Coming towards us! Can you see?" exclaimed Astra. "Is it Eirra? I really hope it's Eirra…"

There was definitely someone flying towards them, but in the darkness, Zoe couldn't quite make out who it was.

Astra reared up in alarm. "Oh no…" she said. "Oh no…"

"What?" cried Zoe. "Is it Orion?"

"Worse than that. This one doesn't look like it has a horn, does it?"

Zoe narrowed her eyes. "You're right, I can't see one."

"What if it's Shadow? He matches all the descriptions I've heard – a huge fairy pony, gleaming coat, powerful and glittering wings…" Astra was breathing fast now as fear shot through her. "Right. Hold on. Keep a tight grip on the net."

Then she veered off, spiralling downwards; wings pressed against her sides, Zoe flat against her back. They shot through the starry sky, but behind them, Zoe could hear

the pounding of wings and she knew that
Shadow was gaining on them.

She risked glancing over her shoulder and
then wished she hadn't. If she'd ever thought
Orion was frightening, he was nothing to
Shadow. He loomed above them, huge and
menacing, his wings pounding through the
air. His dark eyes flared with anger.

"Astra…I'm not sure we can outfly him,"

Zoe cried. "He's so much faster... What are we going to do?"

"We've just got to reach Unicorn Island before him," said Astra, her breath coming in great gasps. "Then we can free the comet. Shadow can't get too close...the banishment...spell..."

Zoe had never known Astra fly at this speed, but every time she looked, Shadow was getting closer and closer.

"It was a trap," Astra muttered to herself. "If only the pure of heart can capture the comet then Shadow must have been waiting for us to catch it. Now he's going to snatch the comet and fly away with it..."

"Just keep flying, Astra!" Zoe urged. "Fly like the wind."

Looking down, she could see Unicorn Island coming into view. It sparkled like a silvery jewel far below them. "We're going to make it," she whispered. "We're really going to make it."

But Astra cried out in shock and the next moment, came to a sudden halt. Zoe was jerked forwards, and if Astra hadn't reared up, she would have tumbled straight from her back.

"What is it?" asked Zoe. "Why have you stopped?"

But as she looked around, she could see for herself. Surrounding them, shimmering and glistening, was a filmy sheen, trapping Zoe and Astra like a giant bubble. "What is this?" cried Zoe. She reached out to touch it.

But even though the
bubble was thin, there was
nothing she could do to break it.

Astra flew frantically this way and that
inside it, kicking at the hard, shimmering
surface. "We were so close," she muttered.
"And I don't know the spell to break free."

Above them, came the sound of muffled laughter.

"There's no point trying to escape," said Shadow, as he circled them, his wings outstretched, his expression mocking. "This beautiful cage may look delicate, but it's stronger than rock."

Astra spun round to face him, with fury in her eyes.

"How dare you!" she cried.

Shadow came closer and closer until he was hovering right in front of them. He was terrifying this close up – the vast size of him, the evil in his eyes. Zoe couldn't help her sharp intake of breath.

"You two were pathetic really, weren't you? So easy to defeat," Shadow said in a soft voice. "It's over, do you understand me? No one is coming to rescue you. You caught the comet for me and now you're trapped, and there's nothing that can break my freezing spell. After all, Astra, everyone knows you can't control your magic. It's not long till dawn now and then Unicorn Island will finally be mine."

Chapter Seven

Astra sank to the floor of their strange cage, folding her wings, exhausted. Zoe had never seen her so defeated. She leaned down to wrap her arms around Astra's neck.

"We must be able to think of something!" whispered Zoe. "A spell, anything! We have to get out of here."

She cast anxious glances at Shadow, but he

had now
flown a
little way
off and was
scanning the
sky, as if waiting
for someone.

"I can't think," said
Astra, her voice choked. "I've
been flying all night. I'm worn out. Maybe if
we just wait here, Eirra will come…"

Zoe began to feel the net tremble and shift.
Looking down, she could see the comet
frantically twitching, its tail flicking from
side to side, as if it knew that time was closing
in and it was desperate to escape. "We need
magic," said Zoe. "Powerful magic."

"*Powerful* magic?" Astra repeated. "I'm not sure..."

"What aren't you sure about?" said Zoe. "No one is coming to save us. Eirra will never find us here. Unless we free ourselves, Unicorn Island will become Shadow's."

"I know," said Astra. "It's just that the only spell I can think of is a dangerous one and I don't know if I've got the energy to do it. No, it's more than that. If I cast this spell, I don't know what it will do to us...to me."

"What do you mean?" asked Zoe.

"To summon up the power," Astra went on, "I would have to focus all my anger against Shadow, for what he's done to my mother and the island. I'd have to make my anger burn red hot. And my mother always said never to cast a spell in anger."

"Do we have any choice?" asked Zoe. "Look! I'm sure the darkness is fading. Dawn can't be far off. We're running out of time."

Astra sighed and when Zoe looked down at her, she suddenly seemed a lot older. "You're right, Zoe," she said. "We have no choice. Let's do this. I need you to beckon Shadow over for me and keep him talking while I cast the spell."

"I'll try," said Zoe.

"And when I cry out – whatever you do, bury your face in my mane and shut your eyes."

"Okay…" agreed Zoe, nervously looking over at Shadow. Then she called out to him, as loudly as she could.

He swept over to them. "What is it?" he demanded. "What do you want?"

For a moment, Zoe felt her courage
fail her. There was something incredibly
powerful about his voice. As he spoke to her,
Zoe felt a strange urge to obey him – even to
follow him. She could feel her arm stretching
out towards him, but as she glanced down
towards the comet, and saw its pure blue light,
it was as if she was shaken out of a spell.

"Why do you need Unicorn Island?" she asked. "What's wrong with the island you came from? Didn't they want you there?"

Shadow's eyes narrowed. "I have nothing to say to you. I'm merely waiting for Orion to join me and then for dawn to break. And after that...let me see...I might just leave you up here for ever."

Zoe could hear Astra frantically muttering a spell beneath her breath. She had to think of something else to say...anything to keep Shadow near, even if talking to him filled her with dread. It was his eyes, she realized. If she looked in his eyes, it was as if he had some kind of power over her. So instead she fixed her gaze on the comet.

"I just wanted to let you know that you'll

fail," she said. "Even if you take over Unicorn Island, no one will follow you. You are nothing compared to the Unicorn King. He is good… and brave—"

She stopped speaking as Shadow glared at her and bared his teeth. "Of course I don't have to leave you trapped up here," he said. "I could get rid of you altogether…"

Zoe gripped onto Astra, terrified Shadow was about to strike. But just then, the little unicorn cried out. Zoe buried her face in Astra's mane and closed her eyes tightly. There was a loud bang, followed by a blinding flash of light. Even from behind her closed eyelids, Zoe could feel the power of the spell. A moment later, Astra was flying once more, diving back down towards Unicorn Island, as Zoe gripped tightly.

"What's going on?" whispered Zoe. "Can I open my eyes?"

"Yes," Astra replied. "I think it's safe now."

Zoe opened them and realized the shimmering bubble had disappeared. Gazing back, she could see Shadow turning this way and that, crying out in pain. Around him there flickered a strange cloud of light, which grew dimmer even as she watched.

"What did you do?" asked Zoe.

"An illuminatrix spell," said Astra, her voice curiously flat. "It burst the bubble, but it also created a light so bright it would blind anyone who didn't shield their eyes. Not for ever…but long enough for us to escape."

Zoe looked at Astra in awe. "I had no idea you could do something so powerful…"

But her thoughts were cut short when she realized Shadow was coming after them.

"Oh no!" Zoe cried out in dismay. "He's following. How can that be?"

"Can he see yet?" asked Astra, who was focusing all her energies on reaching the island.

"I don't think so," said Zoe, keeping her

gaze fixed on Shadow. "His eyes are shut. I think he's just following us blindly."

"Then he'll be following our voices," said Astra.

After that they dived on in silence, once again plummeting through the stars until the towering peaks of the White Mountains came into view. But it was as if Shadow could sense their presence, or hear the rushing of the wind as they flew, because he was edging ever closer.

"We just have to get near enough to the island for the banishment spell to work," said Astra.

"I don't think we're going to make it," cried Zoe. Shadow was so close now, almost in touching distance.

His eyes were open now and, for a moment,

Shadow looked straight at her, his eyes staring blankly. Then he stopped abruptly, just brushing against Astra's side, and was gone.

Zoe heard Astra's sigh of relief. "The king's banishment spell...it saved us. Just in time! Shadow must have been pushed back towards the stars."

"So we've done it?" asked Zoe. "We've really done it?"

"I think we have," said Astra.

They were both too exhausted to cheer. Astra sped past the mountains, down, down towards the valley floor, until at last they landed in a flurry of snow, right back where they'd first begun – at the Frost Fair, beneath the castle walls. Zoe slid from her friend's back, looking around. She saw the frozen unicorns, still glittering like beautiful ice statues. In their midst was Eirra, who had been anxiously waiting for them. He came galloping over.

"Oh, thank goodness," he said. "I was about to come and search for you again. I fought off Orion and then didn't know whether to come after you or meet you back here. I was worried if I looked for you, I might spend for ever searching the sky."

"We…we took so long…because we had to fight Shadow," said Astra, still catching her breath.

Eirra gasped. "Shadow came for you?" he said. "However did you escape?"

Before either of them could answer, he

carried on: "Oh no! Dawn is breaking. Quick – release the comet."

Zoe looked up to see the first light breaking through the clouds, slicing through the darkness. What if they were already too late? With trembling hands, she shook the comet free from the net, marvelling as it rose above her, shimmering and sparkling.

"Go, Fire Comet, go!" urged Astra. "You have to save my mother."

Astra turned to Zoe, who could see the fear in her eyes. "What if it doesn't work?" she asked.

They both gazed up at the comet, willing it to move, as it hovered above them. Then, with a crackle and a burst of blue flames, the comet sped off. It shot upwards in an arc above them, touching down on first one unicorn and then another, its tail whirring and sparkling, its blue light shining as bright as ever. They watched in amazement as one by one, the unicorns came back to life. The ice melted away from them, turning into a haze of purple sparkles that drifted on the frosty air before vanishing into the dawn sky.

"Mother!" Astra cried, as she began galloping across the icy ground. Zoe ran after her, hanging back a little as Astra reached her mother's side.

Sorrel shook her head and seemed to wake

from a daze, before she gazed at her daughter. "What happened?" she asked.

"You were frozen," said Astra, nuzzling up against her. "I was so worried about you. I thought you might be like that for ever."

"Oh – I remember now…the snowflakes. They were enchanted, weren't they? One moment we were making ice statues, the next…everything seemed to stop. And there was this creeping feeling of cold…"

"It was Shadow!" said a voice behind them. They turned to see the Unicorn King, casting off the last shards of ice. His face looked grim. "Shadow cursed the snowflakes, didn't he?"

Eirra nodded in reply. "I'm afraid so."

They all watched the comet as it freed the last of the unicorns from the ice spell then zoomed over the island, its starry trail thawing the ice in its wake.

"Shadow must have used a spell from the Grimoire," the Unicorn King went on. "I should have known he'd strike again." Then he turned to Eirra. "And you saved us with the Fire Comet. Thank you."

"It wasn't just me," said Eirra. "Zoe and Astra helped me. While I was busy fighting Orion, they went in search of the comet."

Sorrel smiled down at her daughter. "I'm so proud of you," she whispered.

"And now—" said the king.

But he was interrupted by a loud crackling noise at Zoe's feet, followed by the unmistakable smell of burning.

Looking down, Zoe saw there was something else in the net – a small star-shaped ball of fire.

"Oh!" she said. "I didn't realize…"

"Drop the net, Zoe!" commanded the Unicorn King. "Everyone, quickly – take to the air! It's a star-quake!"

The star was shooting out sparks and the ground was beginning to shake now.

As one, the unicorns began beating their wings, following the Unicorn King as he made to flee the star-quake. Astra waited just long enough for Zoe to leap on her back.

"It's an exploding star," the Unicorn King explained as they flew. "It may be small, but it has huge power." He looked up at the looming cliff face above, and his castle, jutting over the frozen waterfall. "It's going to bring down the castle," he cried. "We have to get out of here. As fast as we can."

"I don't understand," said Zoe, as they flew through the air. "How did the star-quake get into my net?"

"It must have been Shadow…" Astra replied.

But her next words were drowned out by a huge explosion, and then a great rumbling sound. In horror, Zoe looked back to see the earth trembling below them. The ice on Moon River was groaning and cracking. Rocks tumbled down the hillsides, trees fell to the ground. But most terrifying of all was the deafening roar of the Unicorn King's Castle as a great crack appeared on its side.

All the turrets and walls came away from the rock face, and, with a final groan, the whole castle came crashing to the ground.

"I can't believe it," gasped Astra. "Our castle…our beautiful castle. Ruined!"

Chapter Eight

The Unicorn King led the unicorns away from the river – away from the tumbling castle walls, the flying rocks and falling trees – until they were hovering above the Flower Meadows. The Unicorn King looked around, to check everyone was safe, and then he and the Guardians began chanting a spell together:

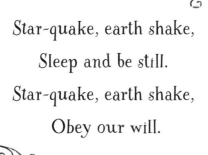

Star-quake, earth shake,
Sleep and be still.
Star-quake, earth shake,
Obey our will.

They kept chanting until the trembling below them grew softer and gentler, and then stopped altogether. One by one, the unicorns dropped down from the sky to land on the quiet earth. The Unicorn King flew across the island, a golden haze spreading like a cloak behind him. Its magical power raised trees from the ground and righted the tumbled rocks.

As Zoe gazed around, she saw the comet had done its work – Unicorn Island was no longer frozen. In the middle of the valley,

Moon River was flowing again, its waters clear and blue. The leaves on the trees fluttered in the weak light of dawn and the snow had vanished, revealing the lush green grass on the valley floor. All around them, winter was melting away into spring.

A great cheer went up from among the unicorns. "The island is saved!"

But to Zoe's horror, the castle still lay in ruins. Its smashed turrets were scattered across the rocks and great chunks of the castle walls were being washed down the river before them.

Zoe turned to the Unicorn King. "Isn't there a spell to bring back the castle?" she asked.

He shook his head. "The castle is a symbol of my power. All Shadow's attempts to destroy the island have weakened me. The castle can only be restored when Shadow is finally defeated."

"Then we must find a way," said Astra.

"We will," vowed the Unicorn King. "We must find the Grimoire and put an end to Shadow's evil plans." He looked down at Zoe as he spoke. "We will talk more on your next visit. The morning light is spreading across the sky and it's time for you to leave the island, or you risk never being able to return to your own world."

Seeing Zoe's panic, the Unicorn King smiled in reassurance. "You'll make it," he said. "But you must hurry. And remember, time moves more slowly in your world, so when you do get back, you will still have some night left. Astra!" he called, beckoning her over. "Can you fly Zoe back to the entrance to the Great Oak?"

"Of course I can," said Astra.

"Thank you for everything," said the Unicorn King.

"Goodbye, Your Majesty," said Zoe.

"Fly well," he said. "You need to reach the entrance to the Great Oak before the sun rises fully above the horizon."

"I want to thank you too," added Sorrel,

smiling down at her. "For helping save the island once again – and for helping Astra."

"I'm just glad that you're safe," Zoe replied, as she climbed onto Astra's back one last time. Without waiting a moment longer, Astra took flight as Zoe waved to the other unicorns.

"Are you sure you can take me?" asked Zoe. "You must be exhausted after our night among the stars."

"It's strange," Astra replied. "But I don't feel tired at all. Instead I feel full of a strange kind of energy…"

Zoe didn't reply straight away. She was too busy drinking in the beauty of Unicorn Island. The first signs of spring were everywhere – leaves were unfurling on the trees, birdsong filled the air and already she could see spring flowers opening their petals across the valley floor. It was only when she looked back at the ruined castle that she realized how close to destruction they'd come. She couldn't help a tear escaping as she thought of the castle as she'd first seen it – a living part of the landscape, its spiralling turrets touching the sky.

"Next time, we'll defeat Shadow for good," she vowed.

It was only when they touched down by the

entrance to the Great Oak and Zoe slipped from her Astra's back, that she noticed how silent they'd been, how Astra didn't look up, or meet her eye.

"What is it?" Zoe asked. She knew she had to go, but she couldn't bear to drag herself away. "Is something wrong, Astra?"

"It's nothing," said Astra. "You should go. The sun is rising fast."

"Please, tell me," said Zoe. "Are you hurt? Or injured?"

"It's not that," said Astra. She took a deep breath. "It's that spell – the one I cast over Shadow to blind him. I don't know where it came from, and it felt different to any magic I've used before."

"Different in what way?" asked Zoe.

Astra looked as if she was struggling to explain. "I'm not sure," she replied. "Just that I cast a spell in anger, and then afterwards, it almost felt like Shadow had gained some kind of power over me."

"You only did that spell so we could escape," Zoe reassured her. "If you hadn't said it, we could never have saved the island – or your mother."

"I know," said Astra with a smile. "I'm sure it's nothing. And thank you, Zoe, for helping us again."

Zoe hugged her friend one last time. "I'll be back," she said. "I want to be there, for the final battle against Shadow. I'm so proud of what we achieved."

"Me too," Astra replied. She still looked sad, but then she smiled. "We make a great team," she added. "I couldn't have done this without you."

Zoe gave Astra one last hug and then she was off, running down the tunnel of the oak tree, back to her own world. She knew that when she finally tumbled into bed, she would be dreaming of flying through the night sky, chasing fiery blue comets with starry tails. When morning came, she would hardly be able to believe she'd been on such a magical adventure...

Edited by Becky Walker

Designed by Brenda Cole

Reading consultant: Alison Kelly

Digital Manipulation by Nick Wakeford

First published in 2017 by Usborne Publishing Ltd.,
Usborne House, 83-85 Saffron Hill, London EC1N 8RT, England.
www.usborne.com

Copyright © Usborne Publishing, 2017

Illustrations copyright © Usborne Publishing, 2017

Front cover and inside illustrations by Nuno Alexandre Vieira

The name Usborne and the devices ♀ ⊕ are Trade Marks of
Usborne Publishing Ltd.

This is a work of fiction. The characters, incidents, and dialogues are products of the author's
imagination and are not to be construed as real. Any resemblance to actual events or persons,
living or dead, is entirely coincidental.

A CIP catalogue record for this book is available from the British Library.